25 REASONS WHY™

They Won't Hire You!

How to Overcome Unfair Hiring Practices AND Get Hired

ZENJA GLASS

25 REASONS WHY™

They Won't Hire You!

How to Overcome Unfair Hiring Practices AND Get Hired

ZENJA GLASS

OPC
Omni Publishing Company

Unlocking Greatness™

Omni Publishing Company
P.O. Box 7208
Prospect Heights, IL 60070

For up-to-date information about the
25 Reasons Why™ book series, visit
www.OmniPublishingCompany.com

Copyright 2007 by ZENJA GLASS

25 Reasons Why™ They Won't Hire You!

Manufactured in the United States of America. All rights reserved. No part of this book may be used or reproduced or transmitted in any form or by any means, electronic or mechanical, including photocopying, recording, or by any information storage or retrieval system, without written permission from Omni Publishing Company and author Zenja Glass, except by a reviewer, who may quote brief passages in a review. For information, contact Omni Publishing Company, P.O. Box 7208, Prospect Heights, IL 60070.
Published by *Omni Publishing Company*.

Visit our website at *www.25ReasonsWhy.com* for more information on available *25 Reasons Why™* book titles.

Library of Congress Control Number: 2007930236

ISBN 10: 0-9667452-4-8
ISBN 13: 978-0-9667452-4-5

Printed and bound in the United States of America.

Cover designed by Pam Hamilton at www.pamhamdesign.com

Disclaimer: The 25 reasons presented in this book are not a reflection of the beliefs and attitudes of my associates or any company I have represented in any manner. Publisher and author assume no liability for any loss or damage that result from applying the information contained in this book.

ACKNOWLEDGMENTS

First, I would like to thank God for giving me the idea and the talent to be able to write a series of *25 Reasons Why*™ career books. Without Him, none of this would be possible. I would also like to give special thanks to my family. Thank you for all of your constant encouragement and your belief in me and in the success of my books.

To all of my family and friends, thanks for your dedication and for always supporting my ideas and creative plans, no matter how far-fetched they seemed at the time. Most importantly, thank you for all of the love you have given me. Special thanks to a very gifted author and friend, Virginia Lefler, and my fantastic, award-winning editor, Sharon Gauthier!

ABOUT THE AUTHOR

Zenja Glass has over 16 years of experience as a corporate employment specialist, professional recruiter, and business owner serving clients in the United States and abroad. She has extensive training in screening applicants, conducting interviews, and hiring applicants. She has interviewed thousands of people for positions ranging from general labor to presidents of some of the leading corporations in the United States today. Since 1999, she has been the co-owner and vice president of USA Technical Search, Inc., a reputable recruitment firm.

Zenja Glass received her Master of Arts degree in organizational communications from Marquette University in Milwaukee, Wisconsin. While attending Marquette, she also taught undergraduate public speaking courses. In her spare time, she teaches online courses and conducts training workshops for recruiters, account executives and job seekers.

Her strong recruitment and sales experience, coupled with her in-depth knowledge of the staffing industry, have made her a highly sought-after recruiter and leading author in this industry.

We hope you enjoy the *25 Reasons Why*™ book series.

BOOKS BY ZENJA GLASS

Career Books:

> **25 Reasons Why™ I Won't Hire You!**
> *What You Did Wrong Before, During and After the Interview*
>
> **25 Reasons Why™ They Won't Hire You!**
> *How to Overcome Unfair Hiring Practices AND Get Hired*

Relationship Books:

> **25 Reasons Why™ You Can't Find or Keep a Man!**
> *Unedited Interviews & Quotes from 125 Single Men*
>
> **25 Reasons Why™ You Can't Find or Keep a Woman!**
> *Unedited Interviews & Quotes from 125 Single Women*

For upcoming 25 Reasons Why™ book releases, please visit our website at www.25ReasonsWhy.com.

Questions? Suggestions? Feedback?
Please e-mail us at: customerservice@25ReasonsWhy.com

Attention Customers: Quantity discounts are available on bulk purchases. For more information, please visit our website at www.25ReasonsWhy.com.

How to Order:
To order online, log on to www.25ReasonsWhy.com. For mail orders, please send a check or money order payable to: Omni Publishing Company, P.O. Box 7208, Prospect Heights, IL 60070. **Single copies are $12.50 + $2.50 S/H** for each book. When ordering, please be sure to include your name, address, phone number, and e-mail address.

A NOTE FROM THE AUTHOR

There are a few things I have to do in life: breathe, eat, drink, sleep, pray, take care of my family, return my mom's calls, and write this book! I simply could not sleep another night with full knowledge—inside knowledge—of the hiring discrimination practices that are happening every day, but which very few people in my position seem to be addressing head-on. I feel I have a moral obligation to the general public, to myself, and to every job seeker to expose these unfair hiring practices and to teach job seekers how to overcome these obstacles.

Please keep in mind a few things as you read this book. Some of the quotes I have heard directly and/or indirectly. Some of the quotes were told to me (via inside information) from other human resources executives. Some of the quotes were simply inconsiderate statements that I recall hearing over the past 16 years from various sources and individuals in positions of authority.

ENJOY!

Z.

To receive our monthly newsletter filled with career tips and job advice, please join our 25 Reasons Why™ Career Book Club. To join, simply log on to www.25ReasonsWhy.com and sign up.

TABLE OF CONTENTS

#1 Physical Disabilities 13
#2 Obesity 19
#3 Race & Ethnicity 25
#4 Sexual Orientation 31
#5 Religion 37
#6 Nationality/Citizenship 43
#7 Age 47
#8 Gender 51

#9 Pregnancy 55
#10 Poor Communication Skills 59
#11 Nepotism/Favoritism 63
#12 They Just Don't Like You 67
#13 Same Company for Over 20 Years 71
#14 Educational Background 75
#15 Socioeconomic Status 79
#16 Criminal Record 83
#17 Terminated or Fired from Previous Employment 87

#18 You are Not Attractive 91
#19 You are Too Attractive 95
#20 You are Too Honest 99
#21 They Think You are Lying 103
#22 You Intimidate Them 107
#23 Misconceptions 111
#24 Envy 115
#25 They are Trying to Help You 119

CHAPTER 1

PHYSICAL DISABILITIES

SHAMEFUL STATEMENTS:

"If we hired him, we would have to make all kinds of arrangements to accommodate him. I don't even know how we could get him into his work station without having to move things."

"If she doesn't work out, we could get into a lot of trouble trying to terminate her."

№ 1 PHYSICAL DISABILITIES

It breaks my heart tremendously to write about this topic for so many personal reasons; however, I know it must be done. It must be written because this kind of hiring discrimination does exist and people need to be aware that sometimes they will be turned down for a position simply because they have a physical disability. In fact, based on my observation over the past 16 years of working in staffing, I believe it happens quite often.

No matter what we do, there will always be people out there who do not understand the challenges the disabled job seekers face, the incredible skills sets many of them have, and how hard they had to work to accomplish their goals. For some hiring authorities, it doesn't matter—it will never matter! The disabled person simply won't get the job. He or she will never get hired at that particular company. I know it sounds cold, but that's the reality for some employers. From the moment someone with a noticeable physical disability sets foot in the door, his interview is already over!

Hard to Prove

The problem with this type of discrimination is that it is hard to prove in a lot of cases. Think about it, if a hiring authority interviewed six applicants, and did not even consider the seventh applicant, which happened to be physically disabled, who is going to challenge his authority to judge fairly? Who can get inside of his head and examine his decision-making process? This is one of the reasons I believe it happens far too often.

The Real Reasons

I can't count the number of times over the past 16 years I have heard (via word of mouth in the recruiting industry) that the real reason a person wasn't hired was because of physical limitations. In fact, because I am a person that is not afraid to speak up, I have confronted a few individuals on this very subject, and made my stand very clear. I absolutely refuse to be a part of any organization, or represent any company, or maintain any friendships with any hiring authority that practices this kind of hiring discrimination!

Why Do They Discriminate Against Them?

I believe some hiring authorities turn down candidates who have physical disabilities because of their own ignorance and insensitivity. They fear high medical expenses and wonder how the medical needs of a disabled employee might affect their insurance premiums next year. They fear terminating or laying that person off and being charged with discrimination against the physically disabled. They think about the financial expenses it would take to accommodate that person. They also worry about common things that can apply to almost anyone, such as work injuries, poor work performance (in some cases), how their customers might view a disabled employee, and so on.

I hope and pray that many hiring authorities will read this book—particularly this chapter. I also hope that their minds will be enlightened and their hearts stirred to respond with fairness the next time they are faced with hiring a qualified candidate who is physically disabled.

What Can Be Done?

I suggest to all physically disabled job seekers, the same thing I suggest to job seekers who are not physically disabled—simply ask the interviewer if your qualifications are a match for the position. If your disability is obvious to others, assure the interviewer that your disability will not affect your job performance. Brag about your past experiences and related work accomplishments. Proceed by asking him if he feels that you have a great chance of getting the job.

A Message to the Hiring Authorities

Interview the person, not the disability. Consider the applicant's accomplishments and what it took to get to that level of success. Consider their skills sets. Consider the challenges that person had to overcome to finish school, maintain perfect attendance, graduate with high honors, or overcome objections, and so on.

For those hiring authorities who give the physically disabled a fair interview, on behalf of the entire physically disabled community, I thank you. Please encourage your colleagues to do the same.

If you believe you have been discriminated against, please contact your EEOC office.

---

www.25ReasonsWhy.com

CHAPTER 2

OBESITY

SHAMEFUL STATEMENTS:

"This job requires a lot of standing. There is no way he can stand up all day for at least six hours without getting tired."

"I am afraid he will have a heart attack!"

№ 2 OBESITY

I have to remind myself to stay calm as I write these chapters. When I think about all of the comments hiring authorities have given over the years concerning hiring an obese candidate, I instantly get upset and my blood starts boiling. Anyone who knows my family will tell you that not only my mother (who is labeled as morbidly obese), but many of my family members have dealt with this issue their entire lives.

If I could wave a magic wand and bless every hiring authority in the universe to look beyond the size of a person and focus on their skills sets, I would do it without thinking twice. Unfortunately, this is not the case. I believe there are many hiring authorities out there who constantly discriminate against job seekers that are labeled as "overweight," "obese," "fat," and so on.

Facts

Globally, there are more than 1 billion overweight adults, at least 300 million of them obese.
(source: World Health Organization website, http://www.who.int/en/2007)

According to the Centers for Disease Control, 44 million Americans are now considered obese.
(source: CDC Media Relations Press Release, Dec. 31, 2002, http://www.cdc.gov)

An article in a London newspaper stated, "Employers are becoming increasingly looks-conscious." It went on to quote the results from a study which showed, "70% of women who were overweight at 16 and 21 had working class jobs by the age of 30, compared with 40% of the other women."
(Roger Dobson, "Overweight Girls Face Lifetime of Discrimination and Low Pay," *The Independent*, September 18, 2005)

Human resource advisor Nicole Andrade has stated, "For some reason, many employers equate weight with productivity and laziness. Psychologists have even proved that overweight people have less employment opportunities simply because they are overweight."
(source: http://blog.laborlawcenter.com)

Why Do They Discriminate Against Them?

Some hiring authorities discriminate against obese job seekers for some of the same reasons they discriminate against someone with a physical disability—ignorance and insensitivity. They are afraid of the medical expenses this person might bring (such as, heart attack, diabetes, gastric bypass surgery, and so on). They think the obese candidate cannot stand or sit for long periods of time. They feel an overweight employee might harm the company image. I have even heard of hiring authorities complaining about body odor. Many people feel that being overweight is a direct link to laziness and low productivity.

I remember once when an HR professional was very upset because a different hiring executive stated that she would never hire someone overweight because she felt that they are all lazy and full of excuses. To her, anyone who would carry around that much extra weight could not possibly be an effective employee. When I heard about this comment, it really broke my heart. Of course, I have been in the staffing industry for many years, and you would think that I wouldn't be hurt by such comments. I must tell you, it hurts every time. A cold heart never feels warm.

A Message to the Hiring Authorities

Interview the person, not their weight. I remember a candidate we assisted by helping him find employment. He was out of work for quite some time, and by the time he came to us, you could tell he felt defeated. He could not understand why someone with his skills could not find a job. I did not have to talk with him about why this could be happening. He knew that his body size was the primary reason he was being turned away. We sent him to one of our clients, and with very little convincing, he was hired. He quickly became one of the most reliable and diligent contract employees we ever hired. His job required standing all day. Not only was he dependable, he was one of the fastest and most positive people in that position. I remember him thanking us over and over again with tears in his eyes. That's priceless!

What Can Be Done?

Did you know that, in general, obesity itself is not a disability protected under the anti-discrimination laws? The Americans with Disabilities Act protects morbid or severe obesity as a disability, but only when those conditions are caused by a physiological disorder or impairment. There are, however, some exceptions. Therefore, if you feel you have been denied employment because of obesity, contact your local Equal Employment Opportunity office for further advice.

It hurts me to have to give this advice, but I would not be helping you if I did not. I suggest a few things. First of all, always look your best when you are going on an interview. This advice applies to everyone. Secondly, don't wear tight-fitting clothes that are a size too small. As with anyone, that does not look appealing. Third, if, for example, you are applying for a position that requires fast-paced work, tell the interviewer how well you did in a similar position and boast about your abilities to complete your work on time, or maybe even ahead of schedule. For example, statements like the following can be very helpful:

"Out of 100 representatives, I was always the first or second person to complete my duties and be on to the next task."

"I received a bonus every month for exceeding my goals."

"We had to constantly keep moving and load the trucks as quickly as they came in. Here are some reviews from my former supervisors."

"I was the manager for six years. I never had a negative review or any disciplinary actions against me for poor work performance."

Do your best to remove any doubt the interviewer may have about you. Assume she may have concerns, and address those concerns head-on. Job seekers who are successful at doing this can greatly increase their chances of getting hired.

If you believe you have been discriminated against, please contact your EEOC office.

---

www.25ReasonsWhy.com

CHAPTER 3

RACE & ETHNICITY

SHAMEFUL STATEMENTS:

"I don't want any Asians because they are taking all of our business away."

"Black people and white people are too lazy. They don't want to work. I only want Polish or Spanish guys."

№ 3 RACE & ETHNICITY

Well, if you looked on the back cover of this book, you might have noticed from my photo that I am an African-American woman. Here we go again, another chapter that affects me personally. It is common to use the words race and ethnicity interchangeably; however, they have two subtly different meanings. Race typically refers to the physical characteristics such as skin color, hair color or texture, facial features, etc., that may be common to a particular group of people. Ethnicity refers to the national, religious, linguistic or cultural background common to a particular group of people.

Why Do They Discriminate Against Them?

Of course some hiring authorities discriminate against a person on the basis of race and ethnicity. This has been happening for many, many years to people of all races. However, I am still amazed that some hiring authorities, CEOs, and business executives are ignorant enough to make discriminatory remarks so openly.

I remember having an argument with a hiring executive because he refused to consider one of my qualified job applicants because he stated that he could not "trust her." I thought for a second that I was in the twilight zone. I remember thinking to myself, "He is looking right at me. I am not a light-skinned African-American. Surely he knows I am black." After that thought, and a few more bold comments from him, I felt I had no choice but to go over his head to the president of the corporation and report his statements. So what if I put my job at risk at the time? I would do it all over again if I had to. That is how it should be done for every hiring authority who feels he or she has a right to refuse someone a position based on ethnicity. We all know that this form of discrimination exists. Here are a few things that might help.

To Get an Interview Request

I know it's wrong, but hiring authorities immediately try to determine your ethnicity from the moment they see your name. If you have an "ethnic" name, or a name that someone may assume belongs to a certain nationality, you can abbreviate your name, use your middle name, or a common name on your résumé. From my experience, this has shown to help increase the number of calls received for those job seekers out of work for three months or longer. I am not implying this is what you must do. This is only a suggestion for those with ethnic names who have had little to no interviews scheduled within a three-month period.

For example, if your name is Mercedes Anntranique Johnson, you can put the names Merce (or Merci) Johnson, Ann Johnson, or even M.A. Johnson, on your résumé. However, make sure you remember to use your correct full legal name when completing your job application.

You can also use an entirely different first name on your résumé. I know of a lady who calls herself Pauline. Her correct legal name is Poh. She made this very clear when we interviewed her, but at the time she felt that it was easier and probably safer for her to use a more common, neutral name. This should not create any problems for you, as long as you are honest and up-front on your interview, and when completing your application. This happens often, and has now become an acceptable practice.

What Can Be Done?

There is no advice anyone can give to make a prejudiced hiring authority look past your race once he has seen you; however, I do recommend a few things that might help quite a bit. At the end of your interview, ask one or more of the following questions:

What do you think about me?
How do my skills match up with what you are looking for?
Do you feel I am qualified for this position?

How do I compare with the other applicants?
How many people are being considered for this position?
When do you expect to make a decision?
Are there any skills sets missing from my background?
Do you believe that I have a great chance at being selected for this position?

That's right. Make them sweat a little bit. Make them acknowledge to your face whether or not they believe you are a fit for the position. It's a little harder to turn someone down for a position once you have told them that they meet all of the qualifications.

If you believe you have been discriminated against, please contact your EEOC office.

———————————————————

www.25ReasonsWhy.com

CHAPTER 4

SEXUAL ORIENTATION

SHAMEFUL STATEMENTS:

"I think he is gay. The guys would have a stroke if I hired him."

"Some of the ladies feel a little uncomfortable around her."

№ 4 SEXUAL ORIENTATION

There is no question that people should not be refused a job on the basis of their sexual orientation. In fact, not only is it wrong, it is also against the law. For example, the Civil Service Reform Act of 1978 prevents all federal employees from discriminating against applicants and employees on the basis of their sexual orientation. However, everyone reading this book knows that this happens in our society today. Hopefully one day, as the world continues to become more accepting, this form of employment discrimination will decrease significantly.

Why Do They Discriminate Against Them?

Some hiring authorities discriminate against those with what they call, "obvious sexual preferences" because of a number of reasons. They are afraid of what their co-workers, superiors, or staff will think. They are afraid of causing tension among the employees of the same sex. They are afraid of possible lawsuits. Some of them are afraid due to their own insecurities. Whatever the case, fear and ignorance are probably the main reasons behind their actions. Let's face it, some people are afraid of being around others with different lifestyles.

The following is not a direct example, but try to understand the point: What do you think a lady from the suburbs would do if she were walking down the street and noticed a young man coming toward her with what seemed like gang-related attire? You probably guessed that she would either cross the street, clutch her purse, or very nervously observe him as he walked past her. Why do you think this might happen? Because she is not familiar (or does not want to become familiar) with someone who doesn't look or act like the people she is used to being around. This is natural behavior. It doesn't make it right, but it explains why some people have a hard time adjusting to others with different preferences or lifestyles.

What Can Be Done?

This is a very touchy subject. The employment rights of lesbian, gay, bisexual and transgender workers are still not fully protected by Equal Employment Opportunity Commission regulations (source: "Facts About Discrimination Based on Sexual Orientation, Status as a Parent, Marital Status, and Political Affiliation," http://www.eeoc.gov); however, there are many federal agencies, states and municipalities that do offer this protection.

I hesitate giving any advice to anyone to change themselves to become more acceptable to others. However, I would not be doing you (or this book) any justice if I did not at least list a few options. These are only options. I am not indicating that this is what you must do:

- Do your best not to give any indicators of your sexual preferences. Over the years, I have seen a few candidates mess up on interviews by being too forthcoming.

- Do not use words or phrases such as: "My partner and I…," or "I live only a few blocks away with my lady friend."

- When interviewing, avoid mentioning the names of popular clubs, organizations, or memberships with gay and lesbian affiliations.

- Be careful with the information you place on your résumés. I recommend that you either not include popular gay and lesbian organizations, or that you abbreviate the names so that they are not easily identified.

Proceed Carefully

Remember, it is not the hiring authority's business to know who you live with, or anything about your personal relationships. Nor should you allow them the opportunity to discriminate against you based on information you provide.

I must be clear with this point. It is not wrong to disregard my advice and include those affiliations on your résumé. You have every right to do so. I am simply giving you some advice that may help those of you who are not getting interviews, job offers, or have been unemployed for three months or longer to consider these options when searching for employment.

As of 2007, the Employment Non-Discrimination Act, which offers Congress the power to protect workplace equality for lesbian, gay, bisexual and transgender workers from discrimination in the workplace, is still pending federal legislative approval.

If you believe you have been discriminated against, please contact your EEOC office.

---

www.25ReasonsWhy.com

CHAPTER 5

RELIGION

Shameful Statements:

"I can't have someone working in my shop wearing that thing wrapped around his head. He would scare the customers away."

"If she is not Jewish, I am not too interested in interviewing her."

№ 5 RELIGION

Title VII of the Civil Rights Act of 1964 was put in place to prohibit employers from discriminating against people on the basis of religion when making hiring and termination decisions.

To be honest, I don't know if the world will ever get past using discriminatory hiring practices on the basis of someone's religion. While some companies have done a great job diversifying their workforce in this area, there are many others that have a long way to go.

The average Christian job seeker may be unaware that this problem even exists. They may also be unaware that it happens quite often, even against them. It is very important that all job seekers make every effort not to disclose their religious affiliations when interviewing for a position. The truth is, you never know what the person on the other side of the desk may be thinking about your religious affiliations. It is best to keep your personal religious information as private as possible when searching for employment.

If possible, I strongly recommend that you avoid including religious affiliations on your résumé as well. This is very important for those in executive-level positions. From my experience, the higher the position, the greater the chances of religious discrimination practices.

Why Do They Discriminate Against Them?

Hiring authorities may discriminate against those of different religions for all kinds of reasons. They may have misconceptions about all Muslims, Jews, Catholics and so forth. It should not be surprising to hear that some people are more comfortable around those with similar beliefs. Some managers have even complained about not wanting to allow certain employees to take off from work because of religious holidays and the problems it creates with other staff members. Some complain about their Muslim employees having to pray at various times during the day. I have heard of concerns from managers who say their staff is uncomfortable with evangelical Christians. Others have complained that they are tired of being invited to church by Jehovah's Witnesses, for instance. Some hiring executives are atheists and do not like the fact that anyone with any religious background will be working with them. Scientologists get discriminated against as well. The examples can go on and on.

What Can Be Done?

Below are a few suggestions to avoid giving hiring authorities the opportunity to discriminate against you on the basis or your religious beliefs. I am also including a few suggestions for those of you who "share your faith" regularly with others, especially for the managers.

-As mentioned earlier, avoid mentioning and including religious affiliations on your résumé, and when interviewing in person.

-Do not treat your workplace as an opportunity to convert someone or to assemble a congregation. Once you develop a friendship with a co-worker, it is perfectly fine to share your beliefs with him after work hours. However, you must proceed with wisdom. If you make him feel uncomfortable or threatened, he could report this to your superior and spread rumors about you throughout the company. You can also get written up for harassment. I have seen this happen quite often.

-If you are a manager at any level, with people reporting to you, I highly advise that you very carefully avoid discussing your religious beliefs with your staff. I remember on more than one occasion a manager inviting his staff members to church. A few came, and a few did not. Those who did not regularly attend his church service began to feel that they were treated differently in the workplace. They also charged that they received lower pay raises and unfavorable reviews. In the end, the manager was removed from his position.

In conclusion, please proceed with caution. You might have good intentions, but it could turn out to be harmful to your career if you appear as trying to force your religion on your co-workers. Also, protect yourself by not discussing your religious background during your interview.

If you believe you have been discriminated against, please contact your EEOC office.

---

www.25ReasonsWhy.com

CHAPTER 6

NATIONALITY/CITIZENSHIP

SHAMEFUL STATEMENTS:

"If he doesn't speak and look 100% American, we don't want to see him!"

"I don't want to interview anyone that had to cross a border to get here."

№ 6 NATIONALITY/CITIZENSHIP

This is a huge topic of discussion in our nation today. Who is a citizen? Who is not? Who should have the right to work in the United States and who should not? Should illegal immigrants have the right to become U.S. citizens?

All of these questions are being debated by voters, politicians and elected officials. For the sake of staying on task, I will not express my own responses to those questions. Rather, I will discuss the unfair hiring practices that exist and what needs to be done so that every job seeker will have a better chance of being hired.

Over the past decade, approximately 800,000 people per year have applied to become U.S. citizens (source: U.S. Department of Homeland Security, http://www.dhs.gov). Whether they are dealing with these legally naturalized citizens or resident aliens, we will always have hiring authorities who will discriminate against people from other countries and nationalities. It is very unfortunate, but I believe this problem will not be going away anytime soon.

Why Do They Discriminate Against Them?

I think a lot of the reasons are pure ignorance based on insufficient knowledge, inaccurate stereotyping, unfounded hatred, and an unwillingness to accept that people from different backgrounds can bring much added value to the table. Some managers are simply making decisions not to hire job applicants based on irrational stereotypes about certain nationalities.

Some executives, business owners, and managers also may blame the job applicant for negative economic conditions. Again, this is an irrational way of thinking. For example, a manager might say that he doesn't want to hire anyone from China because they just lost 40% of their business to Chinese companies. Chances are, the Chinese job applicant might have nothing whatsoever to do with that situation, but because he is Chinese, the manager does not want to even consider him.

The same can be said for citizens of the U.S. being discriminated against by those living here, but who are from a different country. I have heard of immigrants not wanting to hire native-born Americans because of the irrational stereotypes that Americans are spoiled, lazy, etc.

What Can Be Done?

There is very little one can do to prevent this kind of discrimination because, after all, the interviewer (in most cases) will have to meet you. For many job applicants, it is very easy to determine where you are from based on your looks, the information you provide on your résumé, your accent, and so on. Here are a few things I suggest:

-Obviously, have your proper legal documents. Do not attempt to provide a false social security number, a fake birth certificate, etc. I have seen many people not get hired, or get terminated for providing false documents. This information can, and will, be checked by most employers.

-Ask the interviewer if he feels you are a good fit for the position.

-Highlight your strengths and discuss the skills sets and the variety of experiences you are able to bring to the table.

Sometimes, waving a carrot in front of them is a great approach. I remember once when an engineer interviewed with a company and he discussed his knowledge of a software program that the company wanted to order. By the time he left the interview, they were practically making him a job offer.

If you believe you have been discriminated against, please contact your EEOC office.

---

www.25ReasonsWhy.com

CHAPTER 7

AGE

Shameful Statements:

"He has to be almost 70 years old. According to his résumé, he graduated from high school in 1957!"

"We only want to see candidates under 30 years old."

№ 7 AGE

The Age Discrimination in Employment Act of 1967 protects job seekers and employees over the age of 40 from employment discrimination on the basis of age. This applies to hiring decisions, layoffs, terminations, training, promotions, compensation, etc.

Age discrimination is very common in the workplace. After working in the staffing industry directly and indirectly for more than 16 years, I have noticed that age discrimination exists now to the same degree that it did when I first started in this business. When I first began my recruitment career, I remember when some hiring authorities would make unfair decisions because a candidate was over 55 years old, for example. Here it is, more than 16 years later, and the very same things are still occurring.

Why Do They Discriminate Against Them?

Many employers believe that by hiring younger workers, they will get them at a lower rate. They also believe that younger employees will have more longevity with their company. For some reason, they think that a person out of college will stay longer than a 55-year-old person. Some hiring authorities also believe that the younger generation can bring more innovative experiences and creativity to the table.

The most common complaint I have heard from hiring executives is, "Why should I hire someone at his age when he will probably retire in about four or five years at best? Why not pay someone a heck of a lot less, train him, and try to get eight or 10 years out of him?"

Sometimes the reverse happens. There are some hiring executives who believe that the younger generation is not as dependable, less diligent with tasks, complains too much, and won't stay long with their company. Either way, this prohibited kind of hiring practice is against the law, and should be avoided at all times.

What Can Be Done?

There are a number of things job seekers can and should do differently when searching for employment to lower their chances of being discriminated against on the basis of their age. Consider the following suggestions:

- If you are over the age of 40, do not put the year of your college graduation on your résumé. Save that for the job application, if needed. This should increase your chances of getting interviews.
- If you are over the age of 40, it is time to start dropping companies from your résumé. There is no longer a need to include every company you worked for since graduating from college. Stick to the years of most importance and the companies that relate to your position.

- During your interview, do not mention your age, or the fact that you want to retire in a few years. Candidates have made this mistake many times.
- For the younger job seekers, unless you are a recent high school graduate (four years or less), do not put your high school information on your résumé. If you must include this information, do not put the year you graduated.

You never know what the person conducting the interview is thinking about you. It is best not to share personal information, such as your age. Some hiring authorities have a twisted way of thinking that the longer your job history, the less interested they are because you are one step closer to retirement.

There are some exceptions. If you are interviewing for a short-term position or for a limited contract position, they might not mind the fact that you are open about wanting to retire in a few years. In fact, they may prefer hearing that. However, at all times, proceed with caution.

If you believe you have been discriminated against, please contact your EEOC office.

---

www.25ReasonsWhy.com

CHAPTER 8

GENDER

Shameful Statements:

"I don't think a woman can do this job. I need a man in this position."

"I just can't see us having a guy work at the front desk. That is for the ladies."

№ 8 GENDER

The Equal Pay Act of 1963 requires that men and women receive the same pay for the same kind of work in the same establishment. Title VII of the Civil Rights Act of 1964 was set in place to prohibit employment discrimination on the basis of sex. This act was intended for employers with 15 or more employees.

According to the United States General Accounting Office (source: GAO report, 2003), women earned about 80 cents for every dollar earned by a man. This has remained consistent over time.

Why Do They Discriminate Against Them?

Let's face it, gender discrimination is one of the most accepted and common forms of discrimination that exists today. Why is it that when you walk into any hospital, most of the nurses are women? Why is it that when you walk into a sports bar or restaurant with a marketing strategy that appeals primarily to the male population, most of the servers are females? Consider the dock/loading area in most manufacturing companies. Why are most of the dock workers male?

There are more gender discrimination lawsuits now than ever before. If you even glance at the executive-level positions in the corporate world today, it is no question that the men are still leading in that area. It has become acceptable in our society that certain positions are primarily staffed with males or with females.

Some hiring executives believe that certain positions work best for certain genders. Many of them also believe that the men are the heads of their households and should be making more than their female co-workers in the same position. For corporate-level positions, a growing concern employers have regarding women in their early 30s to early 40s is that these women will get to a point of wanting to raise a family, and will leave after only a few years. Of course, this does not make it right, however, it does happen quite often.

What Can Be Done?

There is only so much someone can do to lessen their chances of being discriminated against in this area. I believe the best options are by getting informed.

- Find out what the pay ranges are for your current position, or the position you are interviewing for.

- Find out how the employer determines raises (seniority, level of experience, skills sets, group raises, individual raises, etc.)

- Ask the interviewer how many male or female workers work in that particular department and cater your next question based on the answer.

For example, if you are a female, and you are interviewing for the vice president of marketing position, ask the interviewer how many women were previously in that position. If the answer is zero, you may proceed by asking him to explain what the previous female candidates have been missing or lacking. Then, use that as a springboard to highlight your strengths and proceed by asking him if he feels you meet all of the necessary qualifications. This is not the time to be timid or shy. You must ask the right questions and get informed.

If you believe you have been discriminated against, please contact your EEOC office.

---

www.25ReasonsWhy.com

CHAPTER 9

PREGNANCY

SHAMEFUL STATEMENTS:

"Why would I want to hire her? She looks like she is about to pop!"

"I can tell she is pregnant. I did not want to ask her what her plans were after having the baby, but I did want to know because I don't want to train her, only to see her leave a few months later."

№9 PREGNANCY

The Pregnancy Discrimination Act was an amendment to Title VII of the Civil Rights Act of 1964. This amendment prohibits employers from treating a pregnant mother any differently from any other temporarily disabled employee. It is illegal to refuse to hire a woman because she is pregnant. Also, she must be allowed to keep her job as long as she is able to perform her job. If she becomes unable to perform her job due to her pregnancy, she must follow the same procedures and be given the same time frame to take off from work as any other employee on sick or disability leave.

Well, I have been down this road a few times. My heart goes out to the expectant moms out there who are job hunting or working while pregnant. If you are in your first term (and not showing), you might not have too much to worry about during your interview. If you are in your second term, there are a few things you must be aware of.

Why Do They Discriminate Against Them?

Almost anyone can answer this question. It is obvious that many hiring authorities try to avoid hiring expectant moms because they fear a number of things. They worry about her work performance.

Will she be able to keep up or stay on top of her duties? Can she get injured or hurt on the job? How long will she be gone during her leave of absence due to having the baby? Will she return back to work after the baby is born?

Unfortunately, both men and women have been found to discriminate against expectant mothers. They both have the same worries and concerns. Personally, I have found that female hiring authorities with children practice this form of discrimination even more often than the men because most of them know how difficult it is to have a newborn baby and get right back to work. They use their own personal experiences to judge what must be true for the person being interviewed.

What Can Be Done?

Well, not too much. I hate saying this, but it's true. The only thing you can really do in this area is to do the best you can to convince the hiring authority that you can be successful at your job, and that you are planning on returning to work as quickly as possible after having your child.

Pregnant women who already have a child have an advantage over those who are first-time mothers. One advantage of those mothers that have done this before is that they can say to the hiring authority something like the following:

"When I had my first child, I worked all the way until I gave birth. I was out of work for only a few weeks and immediately returned back to work. My managers were impressed with my work performance and they all welcomed me back with open arms."

You have to admit, that last comment was pretty powerful. That's why it works well for mothers who have already had a baby. For the most part, when someone has a success story like that, they often get hired. To all of the working moms out there, I wish you the best!

If you believe you have been discriminated against, please contact your EEOC office.

---

www.25ReasonsWhy.com

CHAPTER 10

POOR COMMUNICATION SKILLS

SHAMEFUL STATEMENTS:

"If he wasn't so hard to understand, he would have been an ideal candidate."

"I feel sorry for her because she just graduated from college, but she needs a lot of work. She has to learn how to speak better. I can't have her on the phone with our clients. She will need a lot of work."

№10 POOR COMMUNICATION SKILLS

This is one of those chapters that reminds me of how important it is to be able to adapt to different environments. I am a direct product of growing up in, what some refer to as, the ghetto. Urban slang was my language—my only language. However, as I began to get serious about going to college, I realized that I had to develop my language skills to be able to effectively communicate with people in different environments. Unfortunately, not everyone can easily make this transition.

Why Do They Discriminate Against Them?

Depending on the position to be filled, hiring authorities will definitely use any and every kind of discriminatory hiring practice to keep from employing someone with poor communication skills. This happens all the time, especially for positions that require communicating with customers or visitors.

They discriminate against those who do not properly speak a certain language because of a number of reasons: They want to make sure their customers can clearly understand you. Some of them feel that they are protecting the image of their company by ensuring all employees can and will communicate effectively with everyone.

I believe there are some hiring authorities who use this form of discrimination as a result of their own embarrassment because they are from the same country or area, and they don't want to look bad. Others discriminate in this way simply because they do not like "those" people. They do not like "ghetto" people or "foreign" people, etc. Let's not forget, hiring executives are human. Some of them go to work with the same prejudices or thoughts they had when they woke up in the morning.

What Can Be Done?

If English is not your first language, and you speak with any kind of an accent, please make sure you speak slowly and clearly to be understood. The number one complaint I have heard from managers after interviewing someone who does not use English as their primary language, is that they could not understand the person being interviewed. I know English can be a very difficult language, but you must practice pronouncing the words correctly and giving full complete answers instead of the head nods, followed by a yes or a no.

The number one complaint I have received regarding those applicants who do use English as a first (and only) language is that they use too much slang and need to learn to pronounce words correctly. Unfortunately, this has been pretty consistent with some of the candidates from low-income areas. As a self-test, check your pronunciation with someone who can give you honest feedback. For example, say "ask" to make sure that it is not sounding like "ax." You must learn how to properly pronounce your words and speak in complete sentences with the correct subject and verb agreements.

This is one of the primary reasons I gave examples in Chapter 3 about how to put your name on your résumé if you have an easily identifiable "ethnic name." I don't want you to be judged without even having a chance to get the interview. If you have not yet read that section, please refer to it.

I cannot end this chapter without a few words of encouragement. For those of you who have worked hard to learn the English language, finish high school, graduate from college, or work up the corporate ladder, do not ever allow anyone to discourage you from your goals. Be open-minded to changing and improving in certain areas so that you will always be growing. Don't ever allow yourself to be limited!

If you believe you have been discriminated against, please contact your EEOC office.

---

www.25ReasonsWhy.com

CHAPTER 11

NEPOTISM/FAVORITISM

SHAMEFUL STATEMENTS:

"I am going to hire you. I just have to interview these other two guys just to appear to be fair to everyone."

"My brother is graduating this month. Save one of those management positions for him."

№11 Nepotism/Favoritism

Sometimes, you can do everything right and still not get hired. You can have the right experience, the right attitude, the right education, and everything else. However, because they are only going through the proper "routine" and they already have their minds made up about who they are going to hire, you never had a chance! Nepotism and showing favoritism to family members or friends does exist, and will probably always exist in the workplace.

Why Do They Discriminate Against Them?

I don't think hiring authorities think of this as discrimination. They simply have a family member, a friend, or a referral from a friend that they want to hire. They do not consider how harmful it is to the interviewee to take the time to go on an interview only to be turned down for a job he was perfect for. This is very difficult to prove, except in some cases where someone with less experience and qualifications was hired over a more qualified existing employee.

Sometimes they hire friends from different departments with little to no experience at all without giving consideration to existing staff members with more experience. They can get themselves into a lot of trouble by doing this if employees start to complain. However, if the company is a small family-owned operation, the complaining may not prove to be successful.

What Can Be Done?

Go to the interview anyway. Even if someone tells you that the hiring authority has already made up his mind to hire someone else, it is still in your best interest to go on the interview. Here's why:

- You can end up being offered a different position. In some cases, a better position.
- You can practice your interviewing skills and get more comfortable discussing your background in front of people.
- While you should not accuse the hiring authority of nepotism or favoritism, you can certainly ask him if you met all of the qualifications, and if he could please explain why you did not get the position.

You are in a better position to be successful at getting a position if you already work for the company. It is harder for a hiring executive to give a position to someone outside the company (or in a different department) without offering you some kind of an explanation as to why you were not considered for the position.

If you believe you have been discriminated against, please contact your EEOC office.

---

www.25ReasonsWhy.com

CHAPTER 12

THEY JUST DO NOT LIKE YOU

SHAMEFUL STATEMENTS:

"I don't care how much experience he has, I just don't like the guy."

"Something about him rubs me the wrong way. I am going to take a pass."

№12 THEY JUST DO NOT LIKE YOU

I am convinced that when someone interviews for a position, if the person conducting the interview likes the candidate, he will do everything possible to get him hired. If on the other hand, he does not like the candidate, regardless of whether or not the candidate meets all of the requirements for the position, he will not move forward with an offer unless he is desperate to find someone or is forced to do so.

Why Do They Discriminate Against Them?

In my book, *25 Reasons Why™ I Won't Hire You!*, I discuss this topic in great detail. People do not like hiring people they don't like or have some kind of a connection with. It is a known fact that people like hiring people they like. No one wants to hire an individual that they can't stand talking to. This is why it is very important to have a great personality and show a lighter side of yourself when interviewing.

Some managers fear that by hiring applicants with bad attitudes or poor personal communication skills, it will disrupt what they are trying to build on the floor—a great team-building environment. The last thing they want to do is hire someone who is going to cause problems or not be accepted by the others. This is key for sales teams or for work environments that require everyone to work closely together to achieve goals.

Job seekers who are business executives and senior-level corporate officials have a hard time grasping this concept. Many of them tend to be very serious and analytical with their answers. This is why so many of them find themselves out of work for six months to sometimes a year or longer when searching for employment. Some of them do not know how loosen up a little bit and be engaging in a conversation. Whenever I have had the opportunity to coach them on their interviewing skills, I have been pretty successful at helping them to understand how important their body language (non-verbal communication) is, along with their actual verbal communication skills.

What Can Be Done?

Aside from the tips I mentioned in the above paragraph, I recommend the following:

- Learn to pick up on the interests your interviewer may have. For example, if the interviewer has golf trophies in his office, explore that topic a little bit in the conversation.

- Get a little personal about your life (not too personal). For example, it is fine for you to mention that you are married, especially if the interviewer is wearing a wedding band. Let him in your life a little bit so that he knows there is more to you than the résumé sitting in front of him.

- Laugh or smile a little. Don't be so serious that you come across as all work and no play. I am not saying that you should turn into a comedian, but I would recommend that you lighten up a little and make the interviewer feel that you are the kind of person he could see himself going out with after work hours to golf or hang out.

I know this advice may sound a little awkward, but trust me. People want to hire those that they want to be around. This is especially true at the corporate level. Relationship building is a key factor for their success. They figure, if they don't like you, their clients won't like you. If they like you, maybe their clients will as well. Good luck.

If you believe you have been discriminated against, please contact your EEOC office.

---

www.25ReasonsWhy.com

Chapter 13

SAME COMPANY FOR OVER 20 YEARS

Shameful Statements:

"He is probably stuck in his ways of doing things. I need someone that is willing to learn something new."

"I am not interested in her because she has been doing the exact same thing for almost 20 years. People like her have a hard time adjusting to different environments."

№13 SAME COMPANY FOR OVER 20 YEARS

Years ago, it used to be such an honor to see job applicants that stayed with the same company for 20 or 30 years. Hiring executives saw them as a valued, dedicated, team player with years of wonderful experience their company could benefit from. Nowadays, that is not the case with every hiring authority. While some still hold to this thought (as do I), there is now a younger generation of hiring executives who view this differently.

Why Do They Discriminate Against Them?

Some hiring authorities automatically assume that your experience or your way of doing things is outdated. They believe you have developed such a routine way of doing things, that it will be almost impossible to train you or show you a different approach. They sometimes assume that you are technically behind on the latest software, techniques, or industry changes. This is why it is important that you follow my advice, which will be given later in this chapter.

I believe many managers are often intimidated by people with more experience than themselves. You have to be very careful with how you interview with those of lesser experience. This section will be discussed more in Chapter 22.

Department managers have concerns about the number of complaints that come from some individuals with many years of experience at a different company. I must say, I have noticed this as well. For example, if a mechanic or a manager is used to following a particular set of procedural guidelines, and she sees someone doing things differently, she might get upset and complain that others are violating safety standards or guidelines and refuse to follow different rules and regulations.

What Can Be Done?

There are a few things that every job applicant with 20 or more years of experience must do to increase his chances of gaining employment.

- Stay informed and educated with the latest technology, software programs, and industry changes. Do not allow yourself to be limited by falling behind.
- Be open-minded when working in a new environment. Expect that things will be different, rules will change, and procedures will not be the same.

- You must list on your résumé the classes, certifications, and anything else you have done to keep up with the latest trends in your industry.
- You must discuss those accomplishments during your interview.
- If you have worked in multiple positions at your company, section your résumé by date with the different job titles you held.

I have found that the above recommendations have made a huge difference in interviews for those applicants with 20 or more years of experience at the same company. Good luck.

If you believe you have been discriminated against, please contact your EEOC office.

www.25ReasonsWhy.com

CHAPTER 14

EDUCATIONAL BACKGROUND

SHAMEFUL STATEMENTS:

"I don't consider anyone with a degree from another country as having a real degree."

"We only want to see graduates from Ivy League colleges."

№14 EDUCATIONAL BACKGROUND

I am surprised that there are still a lot of hiring authorities out there who prefer candidates from certain colleges or universities. It's unfortunate, but this form of discrimination does exist, and there is not too much that can be done about it because it is very hard to prove.

Why Do They Discriminate Against Them?

For some reason, some hiring authorities feel that if a person comes from a certain college or university, his educational knowledge is higher when compared to someone from a different campus. This can't always be true. For example, there are graduates from state universities who are much smarter and get better grades and have a better understanding of their field than a graduate from Harvard University. In fact, some graduates from Ivy League colleges and preferred universities barely graduate at all.

Some hiring authorities also like the idea of hiring someone who is from their alma mater. They like the fact that someone graduated from the same university as they did. It does something for their egos.

There are also some stereotypes associated with candidates who have received their degrees from other countries, community colleges or online non-traditional classroom settings. They assume they do not have the same level of education. Not only is this unfair, but in many cases, I have found that they were wrong. People have to work just as hard, if not harder in non-traditional educational settings or in other countries.

What Can Be Done?

There really isn't too much that can be done to prevent this kind of unfair hiring practice. After all, you do have to list your college or university on your résumé, and you do need to list your degree.

I do however recommend to those who graduated from other countries to consider furthering your education in the United States, if you plan on continuing to pursue employment in the United States. Again, this is not something you absolutely have to do. This is only a recommendation to help you lessen your chances of being overlooked. For example, I have found that for those applicants who pursued a master's degree in the United States, have experienced quite a few more interview requests in certain industries.

This is not needed for every field. For example, in the information technology field, many applicants are being recruited from other countries because the demand has been increasing, and they need very knowledgeable applicants. If you are getting interview requests and job offers, you may already be on the right track. If this is not happening, you may need to consider furthering your education and proceed from there.

If you believe you have been discriminated against, please contact your EEOC office.

---

www.25ReasonsWhy.com

CHAPTER 15

SOCIOECONOMIC STATUS

SHAMEFUL STATEMENTS:

"I just find it hard to believe that someone with his background could actually fit in here."

"I don't think that was a real Coach bag she was carrying. Also, she had on cheap shoes."

№15 SOCIOECONOMIC STATUS

What makes a person look down on someone because they are not at the same financial level or social level? I wish I had all the answers. We all had to begin somewhere in our career. Some people were born rich, some were middle class, and some, like myself, were born poor and had to work very hard to achieve everything they wanted in life. Whatever the case, this form of hiring discrimination does happen, and there are many things we all must do to change it. Let's first understand the definition of socioeconomic status.

"Socioeconomic status depends on a combination of variables, including occupation, education, income, wealth, and place of residence."
(The New Dictionary of Cultural Literacy, Third Edition. 2002.)

Why Do They Discriminate Against Them?

Some hiring authorities discriminate against people of lower socioeconomic status because they want to be around people they are comfortable socializing with. For some of them, it doesn't matter what degree you have, or how hard you have worked to pull yourself up from almost nothing, they simply see what you are not—you are not them.

You would think that this only happens at the executive levels, but you would be sadly mistaken if you did. Over the past 16 years, I have heard of many examples of this happening on all levels. For example, I remember once when an office clerk talked negatively about a lady she was asked to interview for a temporary receptionist position. It didn't matter that she was making only about one dollar more an hour than the receptionist. She felt she had a higher status level and that she wanted someone on her level to assist her.

Of course this happens in the corporate world quite often. People with lots of money discriminate against others with less money, even if less is still a lot! And even when you do get to that level where you feel you can buy just about anything in the world you want, you will still have someone with more who can look down on you with disapproval. It's a never-ending game. So, don't play it.

What Can Be Done?

Don't play the games! I have found that honesty and humility, combined with a sense of self-pride and dignity is always the best choice. You will get yourself into a lot of trouble if you try to portray yourself as being something that you are not. This does not mean that you should not put your best foot forward, wear your best suit, borrow your friend's jewelry and nail that interview! I am simply saying not to get caught up in trying to make up trips, adventures, stories, experiences and such that never happened just to impress the person conducting the interview.

Every now and then you will meet a hiring authority (like myself), who values people simply for who they are. I am impressed by single mothers, for example, who went to college, got off government assistance, and landed a great job. I am impressed by stories that inspire me to want to help those who are already helping themselves.

I am not indicating that every hiring authority is a bad person. In fact, I believe many of them are fantastic people. You just need to continue to do what's right, and be true to yourself. I hope you all will remember this the next time you are on an interview. I wish you the best!

If you believe you have been discriminated against, please contact your EEOC office.

---

www.25ReasonsWhy.com

CHAPTER 16

CRIMINAL RECORD

SHAMEFUL STATEMENTS:

"I am not comfortable with hiring someone that committed this kind of a crime."

"I don't want anyone with a felony working here."

№16 CRIMINAL RECORD

This is one of those chapters that I could not wait to write. I have been battling with hiring authorities for over 16 years on this subject matter. I feel so strongly that people are not being given fair chances, even when they have committed a crime as a young adult. For some reason, many hiring authorities have a hard time getting past hiring applicants with a previous criminal record. It doesn't matter that the applicant may have completely changed the course of his life. They still see him as a criminal.

Why Do They Discriminate Against Them?

This goes back to what I was saying in the earlier chapters, people have a hard time wanting to be around people who do not share their same lifestyles or experiences. I have noticed that almost all hiring executives who will not under any circumstance hire someone with a prior criminal record, do not have a criminal record themselves. In fact, most of them do not even have a person in their family who has ever committed a serious crime. They can't relate, nor do they understand why or how someone would allow themselves to be put in a situation where he commits a crime.

Some of them also have stereotypes about those with criminal records. If, for example, the person was charged with theft at the age of 19, and he is now almost 26 years old, they still see him as someone who may steal from them. It doesn't matter that at the time of the theft, he was living in a gang-filled environment and was not the one that actually committed the crime. All they see are the words "theft" or "burglary."

What Can Be Done?

If you have a criminal record, there are a number of things you may need to investigate in order to lessen your chances of being turned down for a job.

-Determine if your record can be sealed or expunged. I do not claim to be a legal expert; however, I am aware that after so many years, some charges can be expunged or sealed from the public.

-Stop by your local police station and request a copy of your record. It is important that you understand **exactly** what is on your criminal record. You might find that the charge was dropped to a misdemeanor or expunged.

-Be honest on your application. If you lie and say that you have not been convicted of a felony within the past seven years, and that is not the truth, you can be terminated as soon as they find out.

-At your own risk (depending on the situation), you can offer an explanation as to what happened. The rule of thumb is, "If they don't ask, don't say anything." I sometimes disagree with this statement. Use your own discretion as you see fit.

I remember a 40-year-old man who said, "I was young and stupid at the time. I cannot erase the past. I have moved on with my life. My background has been clean since. I am now married and as you can see, have maintained an excellent work history." He got hired each time with that statement. You do have to be careful. I am not saying that this should be done in all cases. Proceed with caution!

Some experts have recommended that for serious offenders, especially for those who have recently served time for a crime, you write, "ask" or "will discuss in interview" on the application under the criminal record section. They figure that you will at least have a better chance once you are able to meet the interviewer and tell your story.

If you believe you have been discriminated against, please contact your EEOC office.

---

www.25ReasonsWhy.com

CHAPTER 17

TERMINATED OR FIRED FROM PREVIOUS EMPLOYMENT

SHAMEFUL STATEMENTS:

"If he was such a great employee, why do you think they fired him?"

"There must be something wrong with him. Otherwise, they would have kept him."

№17 TERMINATED OR FIRED FROM PREVIOUS EMPLOYMENT

Good interviewers know how to dig deep and ask the right questions to get the answers to their concerns, such as why did your previous employer terminate you, did you receive any warnings or write ups, etc. Unfortunately, you can't always depend on the person conducting the interview to be experienced and confident enough to ask the right questions. The result—they decide for you! They make up their own story as to why you were terminated and what must have happened.

Why Do They Discriminate Against Them?

Some hiring authorities assume that you are the one to blame for your being terminated. How can they make this assumption? They pull from their own experiences. Think about it. If they have ever terminated an employee, I am sure that they believe they were right in their actions. It doesn't matter if the person they terminated believed she was treated unfairly, the hiring authorities may believe they were well within their right to let her go for whatever reason. So, if you are sitting across from such a hiring authority, and you express to her that you were terminated without giving any explanation as to what occurred, she is going to draw from her own experience and assume you were to blame. The next action to follow is simply a rejection letter.

Another reason hiring authorities reject some applicants that were terminated is because they feel they are being lied to about the reasons behind the termination. This will be discussed in greater detail in Chapter 21. Keep in mind that hiring authorities are very skilled at hearing common phrases, and they can easily identify what you are trying to say. For example, you might say, "It was a mutual decision for me to leave. I feel it was time for me to move on." Do you want to know what the average hiring authority thinks when he hears that? They are thinking that you were fired, you agreed to leave after getting fired, and you had no choice but to move on.

What Can Be Done?

Not every hiring executive or even every professional recruiter will agree with me on this statement, but I feel that it is in your best interest to be honest, drown him with the positives, and back it all up with evidence. For example, which sounds better to you? When asked why your position was eliminated, here are two responses:

"I am now pursuing legal actions against them because I was targeted unfairly. They placed a young guy over me with lesser experience. At the end of the day, it was a mutual decision for me to leave. I felt it was time to move on after being with them for 13 years."

-OR-

"I was with them for 13 years. I never missed a single day except when my wife had our son. Each year, I received the highest pay increases they were allowed to give out. My reviews were consistently good. I was promoted four times within the last five years. Unfortunately, the owners recently sold the company and the new owners hired a young gentleman who came in with his own set of agendas. His management style was very difficult for my entire staff to adjust to. When I raised concerns to his superiors about his cursing and constant yelling to my staff, as well as a few other situations, he said I was insubordinate, and told me to pack my belongings. Here are my attendance records, a synopsis of my pay increases and reviews."

I think it goes without question to say that the second response was certainly more informative and positive. It was also believable and convincing. I recommend that you never share with a potential employer that you are involved in a lawsuit with a former employer. That makes them very nervous, and no matter how you say it, they will view you as a troublemaker. Keep that kind of information to yourself!

If you believe you have been discriminated against, please contact your EEOC office.

---

www.25ReasonsWhy.com

CHAPTER 18

YOU ARE NOT ATTRACTIVE

SHAMEFUL STATEMENTS:

"I want to see a pretty face when I walk out of my office everyday."

"I know he can do the job, but I want a good-looking guy in here."

№18 YOU ARE NOT ATTRACTIVE

Someone asked me many years ago if I thought attractive people got jobs faster than those who are not so attractive. I don't remember my answer at that time, but I will tell you what it is now. The truth is—attractive people do sometimes have a better chance of being hired. I know it stings to hear that, and it bothers me to have to be this honest, but I would be lying to you if I did not tell the truth based on my 16 years of working in this industry. Before you get angry about this statement, consider what this means.

Attractiveness is not based solely on the outside appearance. It is also based on a person's confidence level, energy level, personality, and so on. Sure a handsome guy may get a job a few days faster than the average Joe, but that doesn't mean the average Joe won't get hired either. In fact, if the average Joe interviewed well, he might find himself being the boss!

Why Do They Discriminate Against Them?

I think we all know that some people are just vain, conceited, arrogant, and think that the world should look and act like them. In fact, it doesn't matter if a particular hiring authority is attractive or not, some of them still seem to prefer nice-looking candidates over the not-so-nice-looking ones.

Sometimes, they believe that it is good business to have an attractive, confident staff. Depending on their specialty, it could even be standard practice to weed out those who do not look like everyone else. For example, look at the staff members at a health club facility, cosmetic counters at the local malls, beauty spas and so forth.

What Can Be Done?

I hold pretty strong opinions on this subject matter. But first, I will discuss the obvious basics that need to be considered:

-Look your best. Put some thought into how you will dress for your interview.

-Be mindful of the clothes you wear (not too short or too tight).

-Don't overuse make up or perfumes.

-Keep a fresh hair cut, perm, or whatever style you choose.

-Talk with a friend and ask for an honest opinion of the areas you need to improve on. Sometimes, you can become so accustomed to wearing that same loud pink or red lipstick, that you don't even notice how bad it looks on you now. So, get some real advice from *real* friends.

Here are my strong opinions: Love yourself! Take care of you and be proud of who you are and what you have accomplished in life. Don't walk around with slumped shoulders just because there are people out there who are so ignorant and blind that they can't see past the beautiful person you really are. And most importantly, never give up! Always keep going until you have accomplished what you have set out to do. So what if all ten interviews turned you down. Get some good sound advice from a friend or professional in your industry, work on the areas you can improve, and continue on with life. Good luck!

If you believe you have been discriminated against, please contact your EEOC office.

_____

www.25ReasonsWhy.com

CHAPTER 19

YOU ARE TOO ATTRACTIVE

SHAMEFUL STATEMENTS:

"I wouldn't hire her if you paid me. Who does she think she is?"

"I am afraid we could end up with a couple of sexual harassment charges on our hands if we hired her for that management position. Did you see how all the men were smiling and looking her way?"

№19 YOU ARE TOO ATTRACTIVE

I never thought someone could be "too attractive" until about six years ago, when I heard about a few job applicants being turned down for positions. The truth is, sometimes hiring authorities are afraid to hire candidates that will cause a "commotion" in the workplace. Attractive job applicants experience some of the same employment discrimination as the ones who are not so attractive. Interesting, isn't it?

Why Do They Discriminate Against Them?

About six years ago, I heard a few managers discussing that they were afraid to hire a young lady because she was very attractive, and every guy in the building would be in her office around the clock. They were afraid of ending up with sexual harassment charges in the long run. The sad thing about that situation is that she was very qualified for the position and, from a managerial point of view, she was a great fit.

I also recall hearing a story about a manager having to end a contract assignment with a young lady who worked at the front desk in the mail room. All the men in the building constantly visited her. She caused such a traffic jam, that very little work was getting completed by anyone.

There are a few hiring authorities who actually get jealous when they see someone of the same sex interviewing with their company. I remember on more than one occasion hearing female human resource executives discuss a female applicant who was very busty and how she would have every man in the company after her.

The same goes for the men. They sometimes get a little bothered when a younger, more attractive applicant wants a position with their company. This is especially true for those men who are self-employed and have their wives or daughters working for them. Good luck with that one!

What Can Be Done?

There is only so much you can do if you have been blessed with being very physically attractive. If you believe this is becoming an obstacle for you, consider these simple steps:

-Ladies, do not wear tight-fitting clothes that hug your body and show off your curves.

-If you are busty (ladies, you know what I mean), avoid wearing low-cut shirts or revealing dresses to your interview.

-Don't flirt with the interviewer (or the company employees). I know you may think this helps, but remember, other people are watching!

-Ladies, avoid the really short skirts.

-Guys, avoid the muscle shirts or tight-fitting clothes that show off your six-pack. Save that for later times!

For those of you who may be laughing by now, this really is a serious issue for some applicants. Sometimes you have to tone down your presence a little so that the interviewer will notice you and not your curves.

If you believe you have been discriminated against, please contact your EEOC office.

---

www.25ReasonsWhy.com

CHAPTER 20

YOU ARE TOO HONEST

SHAMEFUL STATEMENTS:

"If she didn't bring up the fact that she had committed that misdemeanor, we would have never known. I think we should take a pass."

"He has way too much going on in his life right now to stay focused on his job. Can you send me some more applicants?"

№20 YOU ARE TOO HONEST

Did you ever think you would hear these words? Well, sometimes being too honest about your life circumstances and previous history can be a huge mistake. Everything requires a certain amount of balance. You have to give up some information just so that the person conducting the interview will know that you are a real person with your own set of ideas and experiences; however, don't confuse that with telling the interviewer your life story. Supplying too much information can be harmful!

Why Do They Discriminate Against Them?

I remember a specific time when a candidate was interviewed. She told her entire life story from beginning to end. She had so much going on in her life, and she spared no details. Even when the hiring authorities tried to interrupt her to let her know that she was giving a bit too much information, she insisted on wanting to "tell her story." Needless to say, they were turned off by that and felt that in their line of work, all employees needed to be wise about what they choose to share with others, especially when they are dealing with personal information on thousands of clients.

Some hiring authorities also use this as an opportunity to discriminate once they find out things they never would have known, such as the person's prior criminal history. For example, most companies only ask if you have ever been convicted of a felony. The majority of them do not ask if you were arrested or had a misdemeanor. Some applicants do not read their applications thoroughly, and therefore, they start giving information that they did not have to voluntarily give.

Some job seekers are too honest about their current work environment. They say things like: "I work at a dump. Our technology is old and useless. We have consistently lost customers after every delivery because the parts we are making are bad," and so on. This makes the hiring authority believe that you cannot bring any value-added benefits to the company. Be careful with what you say.

What Can Be Done?

It's pretty simple—be selective when deciding what information to share with the hiring authority. Do not share information that is completely unnecessary. Don't get so comfortable that you share every struggle, every story, and every detail of your life. Remember, every time you open your mouth, you are helping the interviewer to paint a picture of whom she thinks you are.

If you believe you have been discriminated against, please contact your EEOC office.

---

www.25ReasonsWhy.com

CHAPTER 21

THEY THINK YOU ARE LYING

SHAMEFUL STATEMENTS:

"I don't believe a single word that he said. I think that guy was lying from the time he walked into my office."

"If she wasn't so exaggerative, we may have believed some of her stories. I can't have someone like that working for me."

№21 THEY THINK YOU ARE LYING

If they think you are lying or exaggerating about your experiences, my guess is, they could be right. How can I say this? Because I have been around long enough to have heard just about every story, lie, and comment there is. I don't think most people go into an interview with the mindset that they are going to lie about something. Sometimes you get nervous, and the next thing you know, you start making exaggerative comments that are closer to being a lie than the truth. An experienced hiring authority can pick up on this. This is why it is best to stick to the truth. Allow me to give some examples:

Example #1:
I decided to leave the company because I felt it was time for me to try something different. It was time to move on.
Truth: He was fired.

Example #2:
I have been a designer for six years. I used Pro E software from day one on the market.
Truth: He worked only in the summers for four years. He worked part-time for the past two years.

Example #3:
On the application, she stated that she was making $65,000 a year.
Truth: Income was $35,000. Bonus was $3,000.

Example #4:
I worked for them for almost 13 years. The company is now closed and there is probably no way of reaching anyone.
Truth: He was there for three months. The company listed on the application did not exist. The name was falsified.

Example #5:
I brought in over $10 million in new accounts last year alone. I just can't believe that after bringing in that much business, they released me. I feel that they used me.
Truth: His <u>team</u> brought in $10 million. He did not generate a single sale. That's why he was released.

Why Do They Discriminate Against Them?

It's pretty simple—they do not want to be lied to. They figure that if you lie about something as simple as where you worked, what you accomplished, or what income you generated, you will lie about larger things such as company profits, sending a delivery, or violating a safety guideline, and so forth.

What Can Be Done?

Another simple response—stop lying and tell the truth! Stop exaggerating and stick to your *actual* experiences. If you do have a story that might seem a little far-fetched, have some proof to back up your story.

If you believe you have been discriminated against, please contact your EEOC office.

---

www.25ReasonsWhy.com

CHAPTER 22

YOU INTIMIDATE THEM

SHAMEFUL STATEMENTS:

"Why would I want to hire him? So he can try to take away my job?"

"He acts like he knows this job better than everybody here. I don't like him."

№22 YOU INTIMIDATE THEM

There are some candidates who I have always had to very carefully coach and prepare before sending them to an interview. It doesn't matter if they are a maintenance mechanic or a director of operations, some people naturally have an intimidation factor that scares people away. You don't want the hiring authorities to be one of those people.

It is only natural for some hiring executives to become intimidated by candidates who have more experience or are more confident than they are. For many hiring authorities, this is not a big issue. But for some, this will make the difference between your getting a job offer or a rejection letter.

Why Do They Discriminate Against Them?

Remember, hiring authorities are people just like you and me. They can get intimidated by someone who possibly knows more than they do. Some managers feel that those candidates with a higher level of confidence are not trainable. In fact, I have heard this often from department managers. Some candidates who are intimidating and highly confident do not always seem to interview well. They come across as being too busy trying to explain how they are right, or what they can change or do differently. This becomes a turn-off to many managers.

A common complaint I have heard is that the person is not only intimidating, but he seems like he is not a nice person to be around. He is rigid, borderline arrogant, and his confidence level is off the chart. While his experiences may prove valuable, they wonder if he will be liked by everyone. All of these factors are what help managers decide if someone would be a good fit for their company.

What Can Be Done?

If you notice that the person interviewing you is less experienced (or less confident), tone down your answers or responses so that he won't feel that you are speaking over him. In other words, let him feel as though he is a part of the intellectual discussion you are having. Don't simplify things too much to the point where you are coming across as an instructor or insulting his knowledge, but use the right words to make him feel somewhat as an equal. This does not mean that you should not expand on your knowledge and let him be aware of what you have to offer. Wait until the proper time to do this.

Also, it might be a good idea to assure the interviewer that even though you are very knowledgeable in the subject matter, you are always open to learning something new, or a new way of doing things. You want them to feel that you are open to being trained and to learning different techniques. This is a great time to boast about your ability to work well in team settings.

If you believe you have been discriminated against, please contact your EEOC office.

---

www.25ReasonsWhy.com

CHAPTER 23

MISCONCEPTIONS

Shameful Statements:

"Did you see how he kept moving in his chair? I think he is on drugs or something."

"She was sweating up a storm. She must have been lying through her teeth!"

№ 23 MISCONCEPTIONS

The good ol' misconceptions! Here is where a lot of things seem to go wrong on interviews. Many hiring authorities have a bad habit of hearing or viewing a particular verbal or non-verbal message and attaching their reality to it. Instead of addressing the issue, or assuming something positive, they naturally assume that something must be wrong.

Why Do They Discriminate Against Them?

For example, if they see a person who can't keep still in his seat, they assume that he must be on drugs, be very nervous, etc. It could be a physical disability, but because they can't ask the question, they have to attach their own explanation and conclude that he must be on drugs or something.

The same can be said if a candidate has been unemployed for a year. Some hiring authorities are not experienced enough to realize that several factors could have contributed to this, so they naturally assume that he is a bad person, he will get bad references, something must be wrong with him, and so forth.

Another example is when a hiring authority interviews a young man who may look to them like an "ex-con" or "gang member." Instead of realizing that this individual may be the best employee they ever had, they assume that he will be a troublemaker and become unreliable. There are hundreds of examples like this that I can give. I hope that hiring authorities are reading these pages and learning from this as well.

What Can Be Done?

You need to continue to pursue your dreams, regardless of how someone might perceive you. If you feel that you want to explain your actions (such as, why you can't sit still in a chair), then that is solely up to you to decide if it is wise to do that.

I am a huge advocate for addressing issues head-on. If you believe that a hiring authority may be thinking negatively about you, I suggest that you ask the same questions I mentioned in Chapter 3. Then, use that as a platform to speak about your strengths, experiences, and skills sets that you bring to the table.

If you believe you have been discriminated against, please contact your EEOC office.

---

www.25ReasonsWhy.com

CHAPTER 24

ENVY

SHAMEFUL STATEMENTS:

"Who cares if he has a freakin' degree? He doesn't deserve this position!"

"I can't believe she is going to be the new manager. I hate everything about her."

№ 24 ENVY

You may be thinking that I already addressed this issue in Chapter 19 when I talked about being too attractive, and in Chapter 22, when I discussed the intimidation factors and how jealousy plays a role in that. Envy, on the other hand, is something different. For clarification, allow me to give a definition:

"Painful or resentful awareness of an advantage enjoyed by another, joined with a desire to possess the same advantage."
Merriam-Webster's Collegiate Dictionary- 10th Edition, 1998

Get the point? Jealousy is related more to having a dislike for someone who may possess the same advantage you have. Envy is related more to having a dislike for someone because they have what you desire to have. People can become envious or resentful because they can see you as having a particular advantage. They see you as having an advantage over them, and it hurts them (or bothers them) to see that.

Why Do They Discriminate Against Them?

Here is a great example. You have a manager who has been with the same company for seven years. He is not qualified for the director position that just became available because he does not have a bachelor's degree. Here you are, with the same level of experience as this manager. What's the difference? You have a degree! Who has to interview you during the first round of interviews? You guessed it—that same manager. Don't be surprised if he develops envy toward you because he can see you as having an advantage over him.

I am not saying every person with less experience or lower academic achievements will be envious of you. I am saying that this is very common in this world. If someone is envious of you and doesn't like you at all, you will have a very slim chance of getting past him or her and getting the job.

What Can Be Done?

If you were lucky enough to find out this information before your interview (or at the beginning of your interview), do the best you can to win that person over. The phrase I used in my book, *25 Reasons Why™ I Won't Hire You!* is to "begin the dating process."

You literally have to think of that initial stage of your interview almost as a first date. You don't want to come on too strong. You stay polite. You find out the problems, and why the position is still open, and you move in slowly to win the person over. Trust me, I know that this may sound a bit far-fetched, but it is the best approach and the only approach I have seen proven successful almost every time.

If you believe you have been discriminated against, please contact your EEOC office.

---

www.25ReasonsWhy.com

CHAPTER 25

THEY ARE TRYING TO HELP YOU

SHAMEFUL STATEMENTS:

"I wish I could tell him to run away as fast as he can. Payroll is going to bounce next week if we don't receive some payments."

"This place is a hellhole. I can't believe he would listen to all that crap John is telling him. So what if he will make $10,000 more a year? I hope he has enough sense to see that he is making a big mistake."

№25 THEY ARE TRYING TO HELP YOU

Can you catch a hint? It always amazes me when I hear my fellow recruiters or some HR executives say they tried to warn a candidate not to take a particular job, but he was so busy trying to get hired, he didn't pick up on any of the warnings. Make sure you open your eyes and pay attention to everything that is said and not said when you go on an interview. Sometimes, hiring authorities (and nearby employees) are trying to help you!

Why Do They Discriminate Against Them?

Well, this does not really fall into the discrimination category, especially when someone is trying to do you a favor by waving red flags. You want to know the best source for finding out information on a company? Ask the receptionist if this is a pretty good company to work for. They are pretty honest! If it is a dump, they may not say those exact words. They may just roll their eyes and shake their head and say something like, "I don't know. I can't say. Well, you will find out real soon." Trust me, if you get a response like that—run in the opposite direction! I tell my staff all the time, receptionists are the gatekeepers of the company. If something is going wrong, they will know.

What Can Be Done?

Here are some things to watch out for:

-When you walk into the building, pay attention to how the front lobby looks. That's always a great sign to tell you how a company runs its business.

-Observe if the receptionist, or the person greeting you, is smiling. Look around and see if the employees look happy, or do they look distressed, angry or bored.

-Ask yourself, what are they **not** saying? Any company you interview with should have some bragging rights (company profits, sales, large customer base, new construction sites, expansion, etc.) What are they not bragging about?

-Ask if you can talk with any of the employees you will be working with. A lot of companies (with nothing to hide) won't mind this, unless they are not serious about hiring you. Even if they can't take you into the primary work area due to security or policy reasons, they should still be able to let you talk with someone to get a different perspective.

-Ask them about their sales. If you have any doubts, ask them if they are up for sale. You have every right to know this information, especially if you are considering leaving a secure job to work there.

-Follow your instincts. Most of the time, my candidates are never wrong when they follow their instincts!

Remember, open you eyes and realize that sometimes the warning signs are everywhere. Do not be so desperate to change jobs or even to get a job that you disregard key factors that could send you down the wrong career path.

My motto is this:

(OLA)

Observe what's going on.
Listen to what is said and not said.
Ask questions for clarification.

Good Luck!
Please, pass on the knowledge.

If you believe you have been discriminated against, please contact your EEOC office.

---

www.25ReasonsWhy.com

ZENJA GLASS

25 Reasons Why™ Book Club

Hello,

I hope you enjoyed the book! I certainly had a great deal of fun writing it. Please consider this letter as an official invitation to join my *25 Reasons Why™* book club so that you can stay up-to-date on all new book releases and topics of interest. Of course, there is a cost. And that cost simply is your minds—your thoughts—and your feedback on the topics we explore. I always love to know what my readers are thinking, good and bad. Hey, here's another reason to join: aside from the discounts I give my book club members, with your permission, your name and/or comments could end up in my next book! It's time to get famous!

To join, simply log on to: www.25reasonswhy.com and sign up! A second option is to email me at: jobs@25reasonswhy.com and request to be a member. It's that easy! From time to time, I will ask for your opinion on a particular topic. Heck . . . some of you might even find your comments posted on my website!

Oh . . . I almost forgot! You and I both know that there are many people out there who need to read this stuff! Do them a favor by sending them this book as a gift. They might be mad at first, but they'll thank you later... I hope.

BTW... Don't forget, *25 Reasons Why™ I Won't Hire You! What You Did Wrong Before, During and After the Interview* is now available. I am sure we all know at least one person who needs to be reading this!

If they won't buy the book, buy it for them!!!
Take care, and good luck!

Z.

25 REASONS WHY™ THEY WON'T HIRE YOU!

OPC
Omni Publishing Company

Unlocking Greatness ™

www.25ReasonsWhy.com